KARLHEINZ WEINBERGER

VOLUME #3

MEDITERRANEO

AF084420

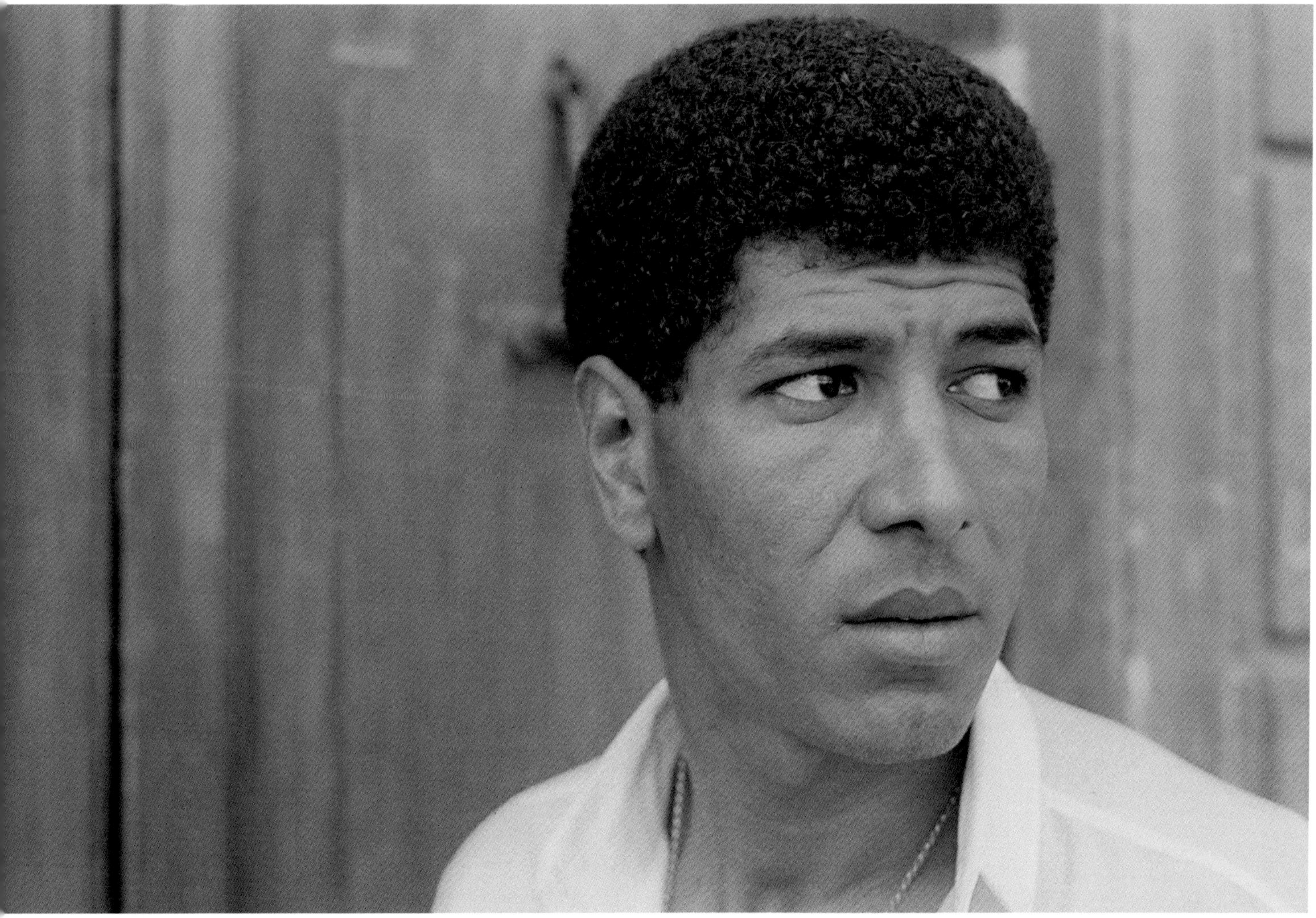

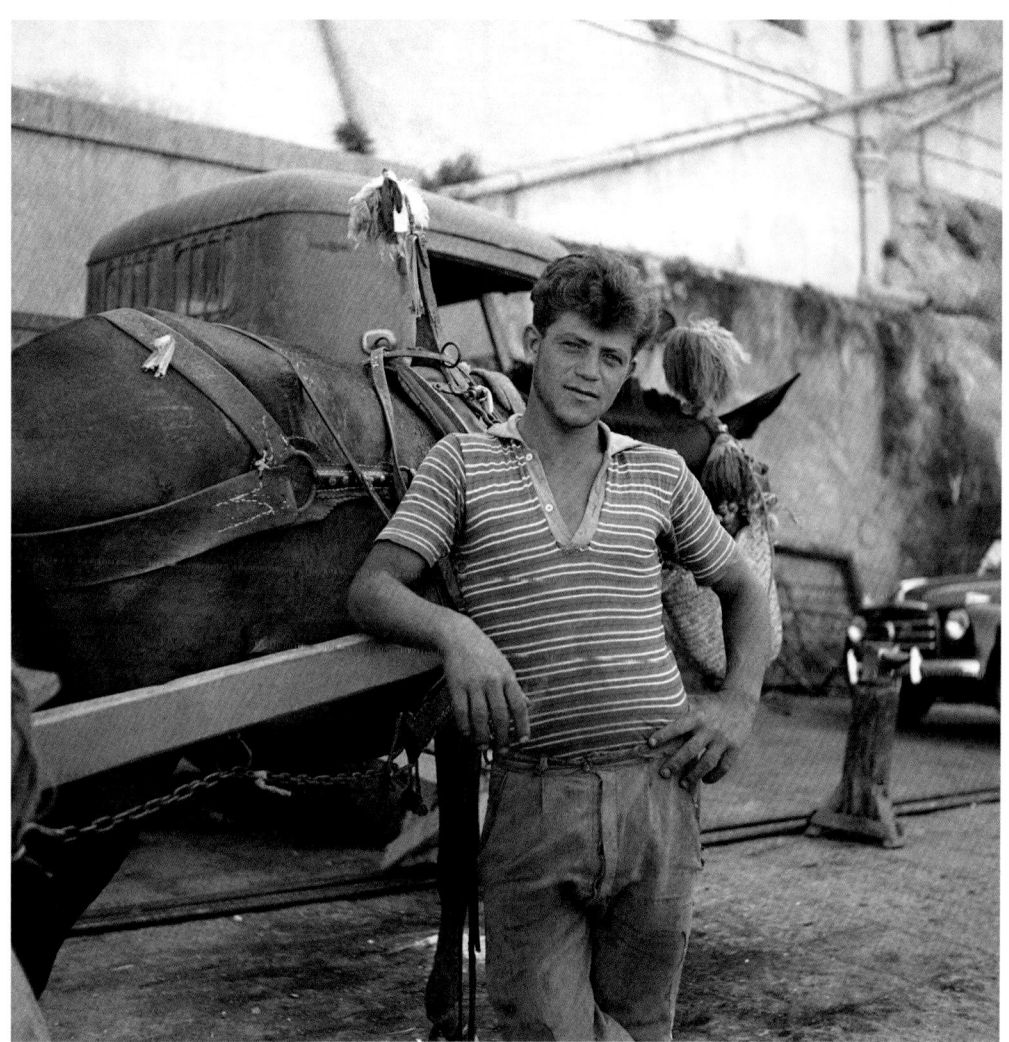

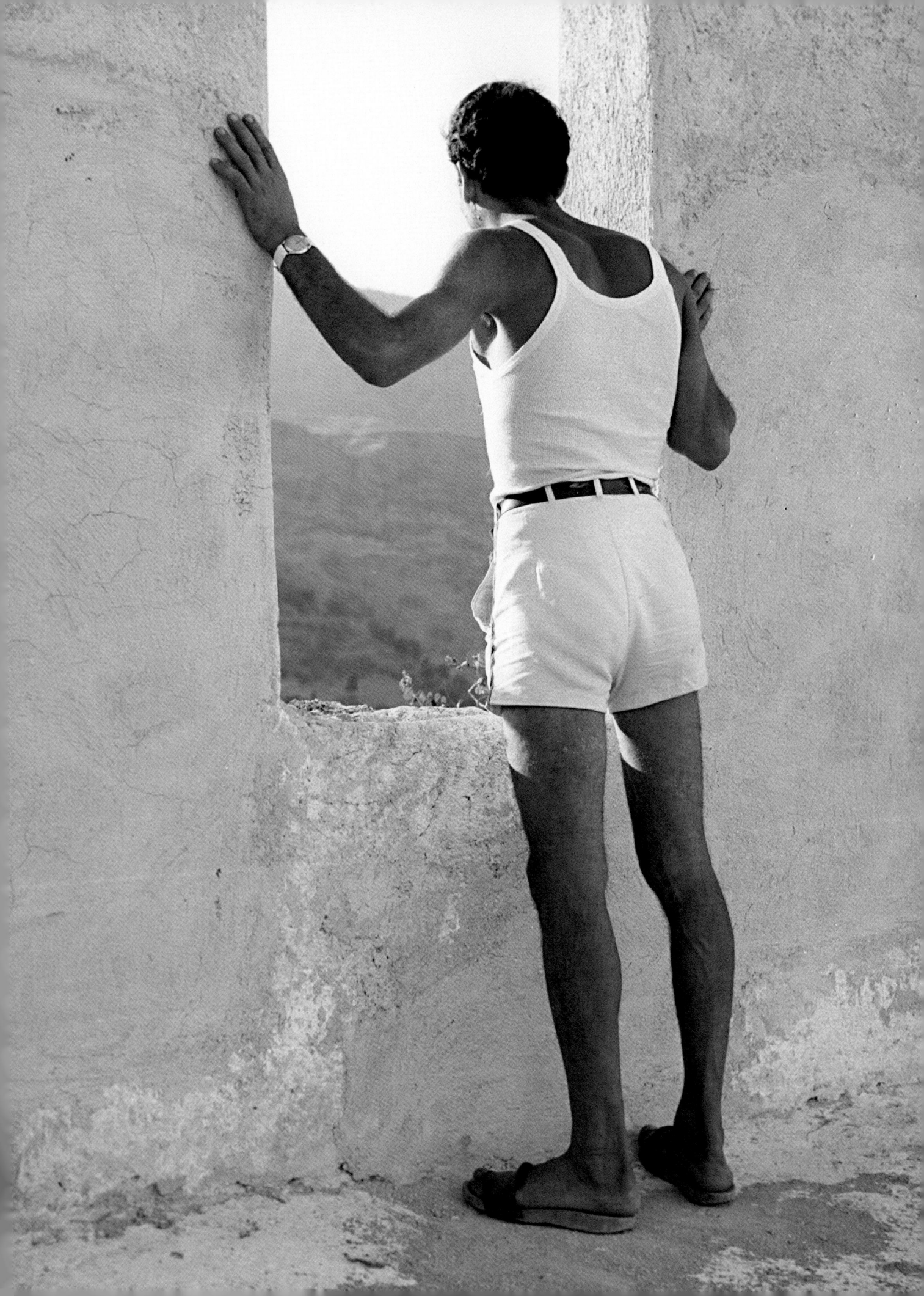

AS HANDSOME AS GLOEDEN AND NIETZSCHE HAD CLAIMED?

The photographs presented in this volume carry a special status in the extensive oeuvre of Karlheinz Weinberger. To this day, Weinberger is best known for his photographs of the *Halbstarke* and of *Rockers,* as well as for his nudes. A different aspect of Weinberger's work was already highlighted in the previous volume on *Sports,* showcasing photographs of wrestlers, football players, gymnasts, and body builders. This volume offers just as exciting a discovery, assembling the photographs that he took on several trips to the Mediterranean. A few of them are well known–such as the picture of the *Esso man,* which has reached cult status–but most have never been published before the release of this book.

Weinberger's contact with the Mediterranean began in the early 1950s in Switzerland. He would visit construction sites in Zurich and take pictures of the sweating workers laboring there, many of whom were Italian immigrants. These photographs form a prelude to the ones published in this book in two ways: first, the workers in Zurich prefigure the type of man that Weinberger would later primarily shoot on his travels in the Mediterranean–men who are muscled, tanned, and rough. And second, these pictures played a decisive role in Weinberger's photographic career: they were his entry ticket into the homophilic club and magazine *Der Kreis.* The publisher of the magazine Karl Meier, known as Rolf, adored the photographs of these workers. As a result, from 1952 onwards, Weinberger's work would regularly feature in *Der Kreis* under his pseudonym, Jim.

It was through his pictures in *Der Kreis* that Weinberger became acquainted with Eugen Laubacher, a successful businessman based in Zurich who became the director of an electricity company in the 1950s. Laubacher also successfully led a double life. In *Der Kreis,* he was known as Charles Welti and was responsible for the French issue of the magazine. He was keen on Weinberger's photographic studies of the male physique, and it was he who suggested that Weinberger travel down South to see whether the men there were indeed as handsome as Gloeden and Nietzsche had claimed. More importantly, Laubacher offered to fund Weinbergers's travels under the condition that he bring back prints of these Mediterranean men. Thus, Laubacher became one of the most important patrons of the passionate photographer, a role Weinberger acknowledged by dedicating his first major publication to him.

These travels and pictures had a special significance for Weinberger. In an interview,

HE EMPHASIZED THAT SOUTHERN SICILY WAS LIKE A SECOND HOME TO HIM.

Many of the photographs shown in this book were shot in and around Agrigento (Palma di Montechiaro, San Leone),